Point of Power

Rev. Dr. Paul Hasselbeck

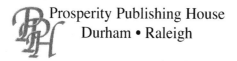

Prosperity Publishing House
Durham • Raleigh

Publisher's Cataloging-in-Publication Data

Cover Design: Cher Holton

All scripture quotations taken from New Revised Standard Version Bible, copyright 1989, Division of Christian Education of the Natinal Council of the Churches of Christ in the United States of America. Used by permission.
All rights reserved.

Hasselbeck, Paul
Point of Power : Practical metaphysics to help you transform your life and realize your magnificence / Paul Hasselbeck.
    p. cm.

ISBN 978-1-893095-44-1
1. Metaphysics   2. Spirituality   I. Title

Library of Congress Control Number: 2006931141

10 9 8 7 6 5 4 3 2 1

I dedicate this book
to the emerging Christ nature
that is the truth
of each and every one of us.

Contents

Acknowledgments

There are so many people to thank who have walked this life's journey with me. No doubt I will probably overlook someone and for this I apologize in advance.

I want to thank my parents, Edith and Jack Hasselbeck, who have showered me with unconditional love through the many challenges in my life. They always supported me on being the best human being I could be and to find a life's work that I would be happy in. Their bottom line was always that I be happy.

I want to thank my spiritual teachers who have walked alongside me, held my hand, and at times pulled me kicking and screaming into being the person I am today. I want to thank:

- Joyce McLean and Raquel Olson who have walked the farthest with me. Their support and unconditional love have been instrumental in life.

- Ken Wapnick for the passion, clarity, and integrity with which he teaches A Course in Miracles.

- Rev. Norma Rosado who demonstrates an unwavering faith and trust in God.

- Rev. Rita Johnson who started out as my minister and became a dear friend, counselor, clarifier, and guide.

- Dr. Jerry Jampolsky and the staff at The Center for Attitudinal Healing where I received amazing training in small group facilitation and the principles of attitudinal healing.

- Dr. Susan Trout for further clarifying and helping me to sharpen my skills as a small group facilitator and trainer in attitudinal healing.

- Barry and Suzi Kaufman and the staff of the Option Institute who certainly mentored me through some decision points in my life and helped me fully realize that happiness is a choice.

- The teaching faculty at Unity School of Religious Studies (now Unity Institute) where I received my ministerial training who helped mold me into the minister I am today.

- Dr. William Freeman who has been and is my friend, counselor, metaphysician, and mentor.

- The former retreat staff of Unity School of Religious Studies (now Unity Institute): Rev. Christine Dustin, Rev. Stacy Wells, and Richard Mekdeci. Their love, support, and many hours of discussions helped hone my thoughts and ideas.

- Dr. Maria Nemeth for helping me realize and gain control over assumptions about myself that had been less than empowering.

- I especially want to thank Jody Drake and Awakening World for all of her creative energy and input in producing the foundation and framework that make this version of this book possible.

- Thanks also go out to Bil and Cher Holton, for their loving guidance and creative energy in transforming my original manuscript into the book you now hold in your hands.

~ Rev. Paul Hasselbeck

Introduction

I have known for quite some time that I would eventually sit down and write a book. For the longest time I didn't even know what the book would be about. I certainly did not want to merely restate spiritual truths. I wanted to be able to add something new or at least a new window through which to look and then apply the spiritual truths I have come to love and appreciate.

You and I are a point of Power, unique, unrepeatable expressions of an unlimited God.

What is important for me is our spiritual practice in this present moment. You and I are a point of Power, unique, unrepeatable expressions of an unlimited God. For me, it really doesn't matter whether I lived before or will live again. It really doesn't matter whether I chose this life's circumstances based on a previous life's events and experiences. It doesn't matter whether the events that have occurred in my life were somehow a soul choice before I came in. It doesn't matter whether I chose my parents before I was born. What does matter is how you and I choose to use this precious, now moment. What does matter is how you and I choose to use our current events and circumstances in our lives. This is the main focus of this book.

There is a great deal I do not know about in the spiritual realm. The journey of spiritual discovery is exciting and so vast that I trust I will be discovering "new truths" until I leave this level of existence and move on to the next one. That I actually move on to another life I truly believe *and* right here, right now, where I sit, I do not know this as a fact.

I am simply writing about what I have found to be true and to work for me. I am writing about what I have learned in this life's experience. For example, I don't know whether reincarnation exists as a fact; I don't know whether there is such a thing as karma. There are many spiritual topics about which I have ideas and beliefs but in the final analysis I really don't know for sure. These are interesting topics to discuss but for me they somehow get me distracted and off purpose. Join me now as I share some of the principles that have helped me on my life's journey. I am grateful to share with you and invite you to participate in these spiritual truths.

My Story

*L*ike many people, my sharp turn onto the spiritual path came in response to an untoward event in my life. Mine occurred on a beautiful sunny day in San Juan, Puerto Rico. It was late January and I was fully involved in a successful career as a dentist. Life was full, good, exciting.

On that fateful day a new patient presented himself in my office for emergency treatment. I had never seen him before and, according to his mother, several dentists had refused him treatment. I agreed to see him and quickly discovered he needed to have an upper molar extracted.

During the course of the extraction I slipped with one of the instruments and stuck it into the palm of my left hand. In fifteen years of dental practice I had only suffered an occasional minor needle stick. This was no minor breaking of the skin. I stuck the bloody instrument into the palm of my hand and began to bleed. With an ordinary patient this would not have been a problem. However, this patient was in the last stages of AIDS. The patient died two weeks later. At the moment I inserted the instrument into the palm of my hand I knew intuitively that I had surely infected myself with the AIDS virus. I remember thinking, "This is it." Several months later, in May, my intuitive knowing was confirmed.

I wish I could tell you that I handled it with the aplomb of a spiritual master. I didn't. I went through the usual questions and torments. Why me? How could this happen to me? I was doing the right thing by treating this patient. Believe me, I had quite the pity party. I was feeling entirely the innocent victim.

Fortunately, at the same time, I had been studying a spiritual teaching called *A Course in Miracles*. And so, I was not without a spiritual perspective. Slowly I began to shift my focus. I began to shift from asking the "why" questions and began to ask "how" questions. I know now that when I began to do that I began to make the shift from dealing with the HIV from the psychological level to dealing with the HIV on the ontological level, who I am as a spiritual being.

When I deal with issues on the psychological level I find the why questions keep me in the victim role. The why questions keep me going in circles. When I ask why questions, I notice that my energy goes down. When I ask how questions I make a shift to the ontological level—the level at which I know the nature of my reality is that I am a spiritual being. I notice my energy rises when I begin to ask how questions. In the case of dealing with my HIV diagnosis, I began to ask in my prayer and meditation times, "Okay, God, now that HIV is in my life, how can I use this to love more? How can I use this to express more of Your will? And how can I use this to join more (end the sense of separation)?" And with that, my perspective began to radically change. I began to see opportunities where before all I could see were gloom and death. I began to see that I could be helpful. Even though the doctors said I only had two years to live, with this new perspective, instead of feeling down and depressed, I began to feel more optimistic and energized. I began to think that if Jesus changed the world in three years, I wondered what I could do in two! Pretty bold, I know.

I began to hear about the work of Dr. Jerry Jampolsky and Attitudinal Healing from friends who were also studying A Course in Miracles. It appealed to me immediately. I began to find out more about it through reading his books and then by going to the center he founded in Tiburon, California, The Center for Attitudinal Healing (now located in Sausalito, California). This center first began to work with children who had terminal diagnoses. It began to create ways that children could openly share about their diagnoses, their life situations, and in many cases, their impending deaths. It is a system of beliefs that when embraced will shift a person's attitude. I list the principles here with the permission of The Center for Attitudinal Healing:

1. The essence of our being is love.
2. Health is inner peace. Healing is letting go of fear.
3. Giving and receiving are the same.
4. We can let go of the past and the future.
5. Now is the only time there is and each instant is for giving.
6. We can learn to love ourselves and others by forgiving rather than judging.
7. We can become love finders rather than fault finders.
8. We can choose and direct ourselves to be peaceful inside regardless of what is happening outside.
9. We are students and teachers to each other.
10. We can focus on the whole of life rather than the fragments.
11. Since love is eternal, death need not be viewed as fearful.
12. We can always perceive ourselves and others as either extending love or giving a call for help.

I received training at The Center for Attitudinal Healing and the Institute for Attitudinal Studies to become a trainer and facilitator for attitudinal healing support groups. Shortly after that, a small center was created in San Juan, Puerto Rico, where I had several attitudinal healing groups for people with HIV.

In October 1991, I had a very intense "dream" experience. I say "dream" because it was not like a normal dream. It was more like that in-between state, the state of consciousness between sleeping and being fully awake. Within this dream I was noticing that a dear friend, Annie Arbona, was teaching A Course in Miracles from a book by Gloria and Kenneth Wapnick that I thought had the title *The Call to Awaken*. It is interesting to note that the Wapnick actual book title is *Awaken from the Dream*, which is what I had to do in order to write what follows. In this dream I was talking to another friend about teaching A Course in Miracles. At that point the phrase, "the call to awaken," began to cycle over and over in my mind. At the same time the presence of Annie was very strong. I don't know how long that phrase revolved in my mind until I finally got up and, uncharacteristically, found a piece of paper and pencil to at least write the phrase down. What followed was much like an internal dictation in my mind. Here is what I wrote that early October morning:

> *My dear one, the call to awaken is everywhere. It is in all things waiting patiently to be seen. I placed it there so that you could not fail to see me wherever you looked. "All things are lessons God would have you learn" because the spark of God's Reality is contained within everything.*
>
> *What you see is determined by what you want to see. If you want death, you will surely see that in everything you look on. If you want death, you will see it all around you and in you because you placed it there first.*

My little one, you do not want death. You want life. How long will you permit me to be obscure to you by your call for death? How long will you continue to seek for gods that bring you experiences of death? How long will you seek to follow means that serve to make my reality less and less accessible to you?

Is it not obvious by now that I am in everything to see? Just set your sights on me and I will spring to your awareness. You cannot but see me in all that you do and say when your goal is eternal peace, because eternal peace is all around and through you. It is all that exists. Eternal peace is your natural eternal state, everpresent, and unchanging. You merely cover it with a blanket of death and separation.

The call to awaken is present. PRESENT my dear one. Present all around you, not in the past or future you project on it. Your projections are calls to death that you dredge up from your past like resurrected zombies to "live" again in the future. And so, your "life of death" goes on in a continuous march of decay and degradation.

I am here. I am here. I am here and everywhere. My spark shines ever brightly as MY goal replaces all the seemingly different ones you have made to replace mine.

There is no situation, no action, no being that cannot but be a call to awaken if your goal becomes one with mine. There is no action you can take that will but bring me to your full awareness if you would just listen. Listen . . . in the stillness of your Right Mind I am calling you to sanity. I am calling you from your reality to return to your Reality. I am gently awaiting your change of mind.

My dear one, all my gifts are yours just for this tiny decision; the decision to see me everywhere and

*in everything. In just this eye blink of a decision to
see only what is real.*

*You must refuse to see the false because the
false is the call to death. All things are lessons God
would have you learn (a paraphrase from A Course
in Miracles, workbook lesson 193). If you feel peace,
joy, and happiness, you have heard the call to awak-
en. If you feel a jab of pain or a tug of guilt the god
of death has become your goal. Quickly change your
mind and see this for what it is, an idol you make to
obscure your Reality, an idol to replace me in your
remembrance. Each experience is either this or that
and nothing more. And that does not exist, so give it
no faith or it will surely lead you down the path of
death and sorrow.*

*Everything contains what I put there or what you
made to obscure it. What you made is nothing but a
projection of something that exists only within your
separated mind. What I placed there is eternal and
extends in all directions and exists in all minds simply because it IS what it IS.*

*It does not matter what another is doing or say-
ing because you can remember it for all of us. It
does not matter what they teach or do not teach
because you can hear the call to awaken. That is
all that really matters. Stop your endless seeking for
little shards of errors and misstatements. It is surely
easier to look for me than to look for all the tiny little
misperceptions YOU placed in YOUR world. Only
you need remember me for me to be remembered by
everyone. Only you need remember me to awaken
me in everyone. Just one—just one is all it takes, my
dear one. Will you do it? Will you do it for me? Will
you do it for your brothers and sisters? And will you
do it for God?*

Do not dismiss the importance of your responsibility in all of this. You accepted it eons and eons ago. You are so close now but do not lose sight of the goal. I am here, gently holding your hand whispering to you that you are as God created you. You are as God created you. Awaken from the dream now and walk gallantly with each step as sure as God's will, unshakable by any form that appears before you. For you know, for we have come, for we have come to help you along a path you but know, that you but need to remember. We are here to remind you of all these steps you take once again as you turn from the call to death to our call to awaken.

All things are a call to life, not a call to death. Illness is a call to life, to life, to life. Live, NOW, my little one, LIVE. Truly live in me each minute and second.

All the corrections you see you want to make out there are just a mere reflection of the true change you want to make inside. So my little one, each time you perceive something you wish to change, let that be a reminder that you really want to change your mind.

AIDS is not a call to death but a call to life.
AIDS is not a call to take but a call to give.
AIDS is not a call to sleep but a call to awaken,
Awaken to your true potential and Reality.

With that amazing poem, the inner dictation ended. I lay back down to reflect on what had just taken place and hopefully to go back to sleep. As I laid my head on the pillow I felt

the very strong presence of Jesus. It seemed like he was strok-
ing my head saying, "Everything is going to be all right."

For a while I did not, could not, share this with anyone. Each
time I would read it, I would choke up and begin to cry. When I
finally did begin to share this inner dictation, I would inevitably
get a huge lump in my throat and find it difficult to complete
the reading of it.

In this amazing inner dictation I can see the seeds of
where I am now in my understanding of my spiritual path
and myself. I see clearly that this message is saying that the
choice is always up to me. What I look for and what I think
I will find is what I tend to find, not because it is inherently
in the event or situation but because it is in my mind. I see,
perceive, and experience my world through my thoughts,
beliefs, and attitudes. This is the good news, friends, and this
is the bad news.

> # I simply did what was in front of me to do, what was obviously mine to do.

The good news is that we create our own reality, our own
life experiences through our thoughts, beliefs, and attitudes.
The bad news is that we create our own reality, our own
life experiences through our thoughts, beliefs, and attitudes.
Knowing this we can assume our power, we can be the points
of power God has always intended us to be, the points of power
God is creating us to be in this now moment. The bad news is
we can turn away from this opportunity.

The amazing four-line poem that ended the inner dictation
became a rallying point for me. I began to engage life more
fully instead of preparing for death. I began to seek out and
find ways to give of myself to individuals and organizations.

I began to truly awaken to the possibilities that were before me. Before this I was alive but I was not fully living life. Finally, I did begin to slowly awaken to my potential and the truth of my inner reality.

As time went on I continued to find ways to serve, ways to love more, ways to join more, and ways to end the sense of separation. Eventually I applied for the Ministerial Education Program at Unity Village. I had never intended to become a minister. Wait, let me rephrase that, I did not have a life-long goal of becoming a minister of any persuasion. At the time, I simply did what was in front of me to do, what was obviously mine to do. In doing so, step by step, I could see that my next step was to apply to ministerial school and, if accepted, eventually become a Unity minister.

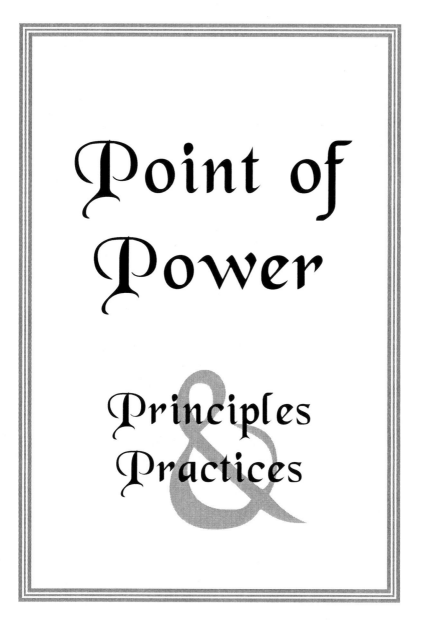

Point of Power

Principles & Practices

Chapter 1

God

The master principle is that there is only One Power and Presence in my life. I must admit that at times my experience is that there is an opposing power. Yet if I look more closely the ultimate power is God. When I remember God and that I am an expression of God that trumps any previous thought or idea.

I have heard people say that the events and situations in our lives are only God loving us, showing up in our lives. Yikes! I cannot and will not believe that the "bad" stuff that has shown up in my life is only God loving me. Now, I will say, that I can *use* all the "bad" stuff in my life to prove that God is love. I can use it to prove that there is only one power and presence. This is not because the event or situation is good or loving or powerful, but because I am an expression of God. I am good, loving, and powerful. I am a point of Power in the expression of God.

> I can use all the "bad" stuff
> in my life to prove that
> God is love.

I can claim my good anywhere with anything and make it so. When I remember the truth about myself I can bring good forth from any situation, not separate from the "allness" of God but as an expression of the "allness" of God. When I do it, it proves that God is all-powerful and good. It is not that God divinely ordered the event! I can use any situation to bring divine order forth. In a sense, as God expressing, divine order is the highest good we can create out of the raw materials of life.

It is said that God is everywhere present, omnipresent. I find it more useful to say that God is everywhere available. This makes more sense, since you and I are extensions of God, there is nowhere where God would be unavailable to us. Given this, and that God is love, here is my working definition of God: God is the Presence that is the truth of what I am that makes every intersection of my life an intersection of love. The caveat here is that this happens when I remember that I am one with God. If I do not remember, then there is the potential that I could react to any given intersection of life with a sense of fear and separation. God is the power and presence that IS MY LIFE (is the truth of what I am) that makes every intersection of my life an intersection of love.

In fact, God is referred to as being omnipresent, omnipotent, and omniscient. These are wonderful traits and troubling traits all at the same time. The issue being, if God knows everything and is all powerful then why does God not stop the horrible things that happen in this world? It might be better said that God is omnipresence, omnipotence, and omniscience. Let's clarify the difference. According to Webster's *New World Dictionary:*

> • **Omnipresent** means "*present in all places at the same time*" which is an adjective while **omnipresence** is the noun.

> • **Omnipotent** means "*having unlimited power or authority: all powerful*" while **omnipotence** is "*the state or quality of being omnipotent.*"

> • **Omniscient** means "*having infinite knowledge; knowing all things*" while **omniscience** means "*the state or quality of being omniscient.*"

Essentially, in each case one is the adjective while the other is the noun. Emilie Cady in her book, *Lessons in Truth,* said:

> God is power. Not simply God has power, but God is power. In other words, all the power there is to do anything is God. God, the source of our

existence every moment, is not simply omnipotent (all-powerful); He is omnipotence (all power). He is not alone omniscient (all-knowing); He is omniscience (all knowledge). He is not only omnipresent, but more—omnipresence. God is not a being having qualities, but He is the good itself.

Another way to say it is that God is the quality itself. Now, if God is not a being but principle, then God would be the very principle of being everywhere present, all knowing, and all power. So, in a way, we might say that when we remember who we are as expressions of God then we have "access" or, in fact, have and are the ability to be all knowing, all powerful, and everywhere present. I know it is a bold statement and yet it must be true. The ramifications are huge. It further emphasizes the idea that each of us is a point of Power in the expression of God! It means whatever decision we are making, whatever event or situation we are involved in, when we go prayerfully to the Silence we have the capacity to make choices from the point of all knowing, everywhere present and all powerful qualities of God.

There is the tendency to think and believe that the metaphysical realm is like the physical realm. It is easy to think that only a part of God's power is present at any given point. This is not true. All that God is, all the love, the power, or whatever quality is available at every point.

It has been said we are cocreators with God. This is an interesting image and still perpetuates the idea that there is separation from God. It implies that two come together to cocreate. This might be thought of as practicing the absence of God rather than practicing the presence of God. The truth is that we create out of the substance of God from which we ourselves are expressing. We are extensions of God. Since God is creating us in God's image and likeness, in this present moment, we simply express the same quality of creating in one seamless flow of consciousness out of unformed substance. This means we are actually creators, not cocreators.

We have the capacity to make choices from the point of all knowing, everywhere present and all powerful qualities of God.

Let's look at spiritual guidance. The beautiful thing about guidance is that it is unique and individualized! This is an amazing and glorious fact. Think about it. When I wake up in the morning there is no way "Spirit" will guide me to take the subway today because there is no subway to take where I live! Given this to be true here is how I think guidance works. We can read in First John, "God is love" (1 John 4:8). When I become still and prayerfully go to the place in my awareness that I know I am one with God, I am in touch with love. I can remember that I am that love. When I am seeking guidance or "Spirit" is directing me, I do not believe there is a being saying "Paul, do this or do that. Paul, take the subway today." I believe what happens is this pure love is "merely" vibrating within me. It is always vibrating within me, everywhere and in everything. As that love vibrates within, a divine alchemy occurs between its pure state of undifferentiated love and all the thoughts, ideas, beliefs, and attitudes I hold. As a result of this vibrating together I see or hear the guidance I need. I am not separate from that guidance. Love vibrates within me; it is me, in such a way that an answer is clear that would be the highest expression of love given the current combination of circumstances to guarantee the best and highest outcome.

Here's another example: I have heard individuals say that God has guided him or her to become a minister. I truly believe that is the person's experience. However, here is what I think is actually happening. God is this vast field of undifferentiated potential, undifferentiated love and undifferentiated substance. *The Revealing Word*, by Charles Fillmore says "divine substance enriches the soil or thought-stuff of the mind. It underlies all manifestation and is the spiritual essence, the living energy out of which everything is made (186–187)." As this person turns to this presence within, which in the most miraculous way is what he or she really is, this love vibration resonates within in a unique and individualized way. God, love, is merely doing what love does, extending itself in its undifferentiated form as it resonates within them. We are the ones that shape it and give it form as creators, with love. People are not separate or different from this expression. It is their unique combination of qualities that already exists within that is vibrating with love. As a result there is the deep and natural desire to give expression to that love. For this person seeking guidance, this expression, this desire to express this love, this desire to give, takes the shape as the guidance to be a minister. This is because it is the highest expression of this love this person is capable of, given their unique combination of qualities and life experiences.

The Bible (Genesis 1:26) says, "God said, Let us make humankind in our image, according to our likeness." I believe that. And, I believe it must be more than that. An image came to me one night while guiding a meditation for my study group, Heartland Unity Church. As I said the phrase, "we are created in the image and likeness of God," an image popped onto the screen of mind of a giant hand with a pastry bag squirting out globs of cookie dough shaped like people. Once it was squirted out it was finished. I had to control the laugh that naturally bubbled up in response to that image. In that very instant I realized that the truth is that God is creating itself in its image and likeness as you and me in this present moment and in each successive moment. It is not a static, one-time event. This is the source of our true power, the source of our true nature.

Each of us is a point of Power as God expressing.

The Bible also tells us that when God created us in God's image and likeness, God declared it was good ("God saw everything that he had made, and, indeed, it was very good" ~ Genesis 1:31). Each of us is innately good not because of our deeds but simply because we each are God expressing. It is because of this innate reality, this innate potential, that we can bring good forth from any situation. It is because of this innate reality, this innate potential, that we can bring divine order out of any event or situation. Not because the event or situation is Good or in Divine Order in and of itself but because each of us is God expressing and has the potential to bring good and divine order forth from any event or situation. Each of us is a point of Power as God expressing.

If we are expressions of God, if there is only One Power and One Presence, how do we go about making this principle real in our lives? How do we go about bringing this metaphysical idea from the level of the mind to the level of the physical universe? There are several ways to do this.

~ Point of Power Practice ~

1. Scripture informs us that we should have no gods before God. We put God first in our lives by making prayer and meditation a priority. Sometimes we put the gods of activity, busyness, money, you name it, before the one true God. Set aside time every day to remember the Lord God of your being, the truth of your being. When we make meditation a priority we are, in effect, saying, "God is first."

2. Give. God is always giving. So, you and I as expressions of God must remember to be in a giving attitude all the time. Surely you have noticed how good you feel when you are giving, giving from your heart with no strings attached. This is why volunteering is such a rewarding experience.

   It has been said that giving and receiving are the same. This is certainly true on the metaphysical level because what you give you receive in the moment. When we give our love to another we are the first ones to experience it. Similarly, when we are hateful to another we are the first ones to experience it. What we give we receive.

You are the point of Power.

This works very differently on the physical level. If I give you a twenty-dollar bill, you have more money and I obviously have less. So, giving and receiving are not the same. However, if I am a joy-

ful giver I can have the same experience as if I had
received the gift myself. Think about a time when
you gave a special gift to your beloved for his or
her birthday. How did you feel? In giving the gift
you were also receiving. You can also be a joyful
receiver. As a joyful receiver you give someone an
opportunity to be a giver. As a joyful receiver you
complete a circuit that maintains harmony and
balance in the universe.

One form of giving is tithing. This principle is
as old as religion itself and still we fight it. In tithing we put ourselves in alignment with what we
really are as spiritual beings. I resisted tithing for
years thinking it was a manipulation of the church
to get money from me. Once I realized that giving 10 percent of my first fruits was about me and
what I am, my attitude changed. At the same time
I also realized that it wasn't necessarily about giving to a church. It is about giving to where I am
spiritually fed. The recipients of my tithing have
varied from a church, to a charity, to a friend,
and to a stranger. My friends, the Reverends Pat
Bessey and LeRoy Lowell, have a wonderful saying about tithing. They say that tithing, giving 10
percent to where you have been spiritually fed, is
the only spiritual principle you can know for sure
whether you are actually doing it or not. It's so
true! We also give because we can. And, finally,
we give as an act of faith, knowing and trusting
that we are abundant expressions of an unlimited,
abundant God.

3. Do not blaspheme God. Now this may be a
   stretch. So please take a deep breath and keep
   your mind open. The third way is to not talk badly
   about yourself. Any time you are tempted to hold
   yourself in low esteem, you are blaspheming God

because you are being created in the very image
and likeness of God. In fact, scripture tells us "you
are gods" (John 10:34). What I am saying is that
since we are expressions of God, then speaking
badly about ourselves is blaspheming God.

4. Call it Good. This means that in any given situation
   you can call it good. What you are declaring in that
   moment is that no matter what the appearance may
   be, there is only One Power and One Presence and
   I am calling it forth now. We can actively do it by
   asking, "How can I bring good forth from this event
   or situation?" I essentially did this in an indirect way
   when I switched from asking all the "why" questions
   to asking the "how" questions regarding my HIV
   infection. In asking, "God, now that HIV is in my
   life, how can I use this to express your will? How
   can I use this to love more? And how can I use this
   to join more?" I was, in effect, asking God to show
   me how I can use this for good. How could I use
   this to bring divine order out of the chaos?

I believe the biblical story of Joseph demonstrates
this. As you may recall, Joseph was one of twelve
brothers who essentially got on his brothers' last
nerve. The brothers decided to throw him in a pit,
leave him to die, and tell their father he was dead.
Joseph was discovered and taken into slavery
in Egypt where his skills as a dream interpreter
became known to the pharaoh. As a result of helping the pharaoh interpret his dreams, Joseph was
elevated to a very high position in the pharaoh's
government. Meanwhile, back in Joseph's home-
land there was a severe drought. Joseph's father
sent the brothers to Egypt to ask for assistance.
The brothers go before Joseph to make their
request and, thinking him dead, did not even recognize him. After some toying with his brothers,

Joseph agreed to help them saying, "Do not be afraid! Am I in the place of God? Even though you intended to do harm to me, God intended it for good, in order to preserve a numerous people as he is doing today" (Genesis 50:19, 20).

Perhaps events do not happen for a reason but we can bring reason to an event.

Now, I don't think God meant for Joseph to be thrown in the pit and sold into slavery in order for God to be in a position to help his family later. I believe good was eventually brought forth from the evil acts of Joseph's brothers because Joseph, being an expression of God AND remembering, chose to use the situation for good and bless his family. He could have just as easily listened to his mortal mind and thrown his brothers into slavery.

Perhaps you have heard people say an event happened for a reason. The implication here is a force outside the person (God) has a reason, an overarching reason, for this untoward event to happen. I would like to suggest that perhaps events do not happen for a reason but that we can BRING REASON to the event.

On the following page is a worksheet to help you with a similar process in your life. We give every event in our lives the meaning it has. So, we can choose to bring good forth, bring a blessing forth, from any event. (Feel free to enlarge this page on a separate sheet of paper to better use this worksheet.)

This worksheet is for reframing life's events and situations. When the events of life occur we get to choose what we learn. Since God is creating us in God's image and likeness, we can take any life event or situation and bring forth good and divine order. Not because the event or situation IS good or divinely ordered but because we are good and we have the capacity to bring divine order to life's events and situations.

Directions:

In the first column simply describe a significant event in your life. Typically, most people choose to look at the more traumatic events in their lives. However, it can be equally useful to look at the positive events. In the second column write what you think and/or how you feel about the event or situation now. Just dump it all out, the good, the bad, and the ugly. In the third column, ask yourself, "What good have I brought forth or could I bring forth as a result of this event being in my life?" Notice that I am clearly NOT saying that the event determines or causes what is brought forth. The event or situation is just an event or situation. YOU are the point of Power. YOU decide what you learn and what good you choose to bring forth. You may have to think, pray, and meditate about this. Please keep in mind that there is nothing that Spirit (you are Spirit expressing) cannot use for good. In the fourth column you get to write about how, as a result of what you have chosen to learn, you now are different or how you show up differently in your world.

Bringing Forth the Good

Life Event or Situation (Positive or Negative)	What I Think or Feel About It Now	The Blessing Good or Lesson I Bring Forth	How I Can Use It to Help or Serve Others

There is nothing that Spirit
(what you really are) cannot
use for good.

Dr. Susan Trout in her book, *To See Differently*, talks about the three stages of life experiences. She says that it is in the very areas in our lives where we have been hurt or injured that we can be the most effective, serving others once any hurts or wounds have been healed. For instance, in my case, through extensive reading and inner healing work concerning my own illness and impending death, I was then more effective facilitating HIV support groups and later serving others who were facing their own terminal diagnoses and death. This model can be seen over and over in the various twelve-step groups. Who is better suited to support and sponsor an alcoholic in recovery than a person who has already been there and done that? Who is better able to be with a person who is facing breast cancer than a person who has already faced breast cancer? I assure you that if you have had a traumatic event or situation in your life and have learned to bring forth good from it, you are well equipped to help and serve another person in a similar situation. You are in effect "calling it good."

5. Express Love. We know that "God is love" (1 John 4:8). When Jesus was asked what is the greatest commandment, he replied, "You shall love the Lord your God with all your heart, and with all your soul, and with all your mind. This is the greatest and first commandment. And a second is like it: You shall love your neighbor as yourself" (Matthew 22: 37–39). These are obviously great concepts AND how do we love one another? How do we take this grand concept, these two great commandments and make them real in this physical universe?

The answer is through our behaviors. Dr. Gary Chapman has written a wonderful book titled *The Five Love Languages*. While the focus of his book is putting love into action in the context of a committed relationship, its principles and ideas are more broadly applicable. Dr. Chapman postulates that there are five primary love languages: words of affirmation, quality time, acts of service, gifts, and touch. These are five ways we can concretely bring love from the level of an idea, and a feeling to the level of the physical universe through an action. These are five ways that we can concretely bring the idea, "love one another," from the metaphysical realm to demonstrate them in the physical realm. *Words of affirmation* are words that affirm, and support another. *Quality time* is when we spend time with another in such a way that we convey that the other person is the most important person in that moment. *Acts of service* is doing things for others from taking out the trash, and washing clothes to fixing the car. *Gifts* is simply the act of giving a gift to another. *Touch* is anything from a brief touch to sexual relations. Dr. Chapman further postulates that each of us naturally expresses love and receives love in one of these five languages. For a more in-depth understanding of this and a good read, please read Dr. Chapman's book, *The Five Love Languages.*

Chapter 2

Indwelling Christ

~ Point of Power Principle ~

Each of us has a spark of the divine within us. I like to think of that spark as the most beautiful fire works display you and I have ever experienced. Scripture tells us, "Christ in you, the hope of glory" (Colossians 1:27). When we remember that each of us is an expression of the Christ, then each of us has the same potential as Jesus. Jesus even said, "Very truly, I tell you, the one who believes in me will also do the works that I do and, in fact, will do greater works than these, because I am going to the Father" (John 14:12). Jesus in no way made himself an exception. In fact, Jesus is not the great exception; Jesus is the great example! Jesus is our older brother and way shower. Each of us has the potential to express in our own unique way, the Christ presence he expressed. This uniqueness is called our individuality. Our individuality is unchanged, unchanging, and unchangeable. This is the pearl of great value. "Again, the kingdom of heaven is like a merchant in search of fine pearls; on finding one pearl of great value, went, and sold all that he had and bought it" (Matthew 13:45-46).

I have heard it said that we are to be empty vessels for Spirit to fill. This is an interesting image and is somewhat lacking. If a simple glass is a vessel and you fill it with water, the vessel is never the water. This image implies a separation from Spirit. However, what if the image was changed in this way. What if the vessel, "the glass," were made of ice and then filled with water? Then both the vessel and its contents are water. This more closely approaches the truth about us. Yes, we are each a vessel for Spirit, for the Christ, and that vessel is the same "substance."

Sometimes people speak of being in the flow of God. This concept brings to mind an image of a stick flowing in a stream. This concept perpetuates the belief in separation. We *are* the flow. We can never be apart from that which we are.

In my work, one of the most frequent states of mind I find is the feeling of unworthiness. This is because many people have grown up in traditions that told them that they were all sinners, will always be sinners, and that the only way for salvation is through Jesus Christ, God incarnate. How else could people feel, if they heard this week after week as they were growing up? Therefore, many believe they are some-how broken deep inside. It is no wonder many believe there is some dark monster inside. It is no wonder many are afraid to express and be who they *really are* for fear this monster will be released.

Jesus is not the great exception; Jesus is the great example!

The mistakes people make in life are used to confirm this. Who hasn't known what the right and noble course of action is and, ultimately, done something else out of self-interest, self-preservation, greed, or expedience? Who hasn't told a lie, withheld information or been unwilling to speak in the face of what was obviously wrong? These mistakes are tal-lied and given more importance than they deserve. They are collected as evidence that, yes, we are sinful creatures: dark, ugly monsters. This is the source of a lot of our problems. This dark ugly monster consists of all that we fear we are. This dark, ugly monster is like a black box encasing the pearl of great value that is truly at our core.

People are fearful that someone might find out about this deep, dark secret and therefore not love them. They are afraid that if someone gets to know them too well he or she, too, will discover that down deep inside is a dark, ugly monster. And, when they find out, they will not love them, and they will go away. They are so fearful that many are afraid to look for themselves. And so, they live for years and years afraid to look, afraid to let others really know them for fear of losing their love and friendship. "If you really knew me you'd leave" is the thought that occurs and re-occurs. So, as a way to cover up this dark, ugly monster, a pretend self, a mask, is made up. It is as if the black box is encased in a colorful box, one that looks pretty and attractive. This is made up in reaction to the belief in the dark, ugly monster. It is a way to hide it from others. This made-up self and the ugly monster inside make up what is called the personality. The personality is forever changing. It shifts according to the needs and whims of the current situation. *The Revealing Word* (page 148) defines personality as "The sum total of characteristics that man has personalized as distinct of himself, independent of others or of divine principle. ... Personality is a veil or mask worn by man that conceals the real, the Spiritual I AM. Jesus shattered this mask and revealed Christ, the true man of God."

When we first rediscover the spiritual path, it is from this level. The personality is always shifting and adding to itself. As we observe spiritual people, we take on their behaviors and add them to our colorful boxes. It is like slapping on a sticky icing of spirituality to cover up the colorful box and the black box. Often this seems to be a necessary step of awakening to our authentic selves. It is behavior that is not based on the pearl of great value within but is based on the personality simply wanting to make up more about itself to look good. True spirituality does not come from adding more but from diving deep inside and bringing the personality under the guidance and direction of the Christ, letting the Christ inform the personality.

Now, this sets up a very interesting dynamic when we meet someone. Let me illustrate. When Jane meets John, each has the perfect, divine self, the Christ within them. This divine self, their individuality, is unique to each of them.

Individuality (Divine Self)

John's
Divine Self

Jane's
Divine Self

Each of them also carries what they believe to be the ugly monster within made-up of who they fear they are.

Personality (ugly monster self)

John's ugly
monster self

Jane's ugly
monster self

Likewise, each of them has a made-up self to hide this monster.

Personality (pretend self)

John's
pretend self

Jane's
pretend self

So, when Jane and John meet there are at least three "Johns" and three "Janes" showing up. It might look like this:

John's
Individuality

John's   John's
monster   pretend
self   self

Jane's   Jane's
pretend   monster
self   self

Jane's
Individuality

In addition, when Jane meets John, she doesn't meet the real John, his individuality. She doesn't meet the John that John has made up to hide the monster. She doesn't even meet the ugly monster John is afraid he is. Who does Jane meet? Jane will tend to meet "Jane's made-up John." The made-up John is created from all the past history that Jane has ever had with men. In a sense, Jane projects all her beliefs about men onto John; Jane sees John through the filter of her beliefs about men. The result is that Jane doesn't meet the real John, she meets who *she thinks* he is.

Similarly, when John meets Jane, he doesn't meet the real Jane, her individuality. He doesn't meet the Jane that Jane has made up to hide her ugly monster deep inside. He doesn't even meet who Jane is afraid she is, the ugly monster. John meets a made-up Jane; a Jane made up from all the past history that John has had with women. John projects all his beliefs about women onto Jane. So John meets a Jane that is who *he thinks* she is, not who she really is.

Here is how it all looks now:

John's
Individuality   John's   John's   Jane's   Jane's
                 monster   pretend   John's   Jane's   pretend   Individuality
                 self   self   made-up   made-up   self
                                       Jane   John

To complicate things even more, both Jane and John keep adjusting their made-up selves in response to the person they are hiding inside and in response to the person they think the other person is. It is a miracle that we can communicate with one another at all!

If this is the problem, then how do we get around it? How do we surmount this complex of selves and others that are really just constructs in our imaginations?

We must recognize that wrong action supports the belief that there is a dark, ugly monster lurking inside. In fact, how could we not believe this if our outer actions and behaviors are so dishonorable and out of alignment with truth and values?

The Reality is that deep inside there is a splendid being, a pearl of great value; a being who would always do the right thing; a being who is strong and has worth. A being who all would love, even ourselves, if we let it naturally express, if we got acquainted with it. It is not dark. It is brilliant light.

The challenge is we have forgotten it. The problem is we have been empowering and listening to a made-up self, our weakest part. This part wants to be right, wants to look good no matter what, wants it easy at anybody else's expense and wants to avoid responsibility for its own actions and errors.

The bottom line is that we do not get a strong life when we are living from our weakest part. We can only dispel the notion that there is this dark, ugly monster deep inside by empowering and allowing our strongest self to shine forth. This entails taking right action no matter what our weakest, fearful self is demanding. This entails NOT doing what is expedient or seeming in our best interest. What is truly in our best interest is doing the right thing—listening and following the Christ within.

We do not get a strong life when we are living from our weakest part.

Being the good people who God is creating us to be *is* its own reward. The reward is a strong life. The reward is the discovery that we are great, radiant beings inside. The reward is a Self we like and love instead of fear and avoid. We dispel the darkness by letting our true light shine through all our seeming darkness. Light dispels the dark. Sometimes this means sharing with a trusted, compassionate friend, a friend who will help and support you to discover and empower your inner Christ.

~ Point of Power Practice ~

The next time you want to do what is expedient or in your self-interest instead of doing what is noble and right, STOP. Ask yourself, "Do I want to further strengthen the belief that I have an ugly monster deep inside or do I want to empower the truth that deep inside resides the Christ?" Realign yourself with the inner Christ and discover that the monster was just something you made up, a belief about yourself that is not true. Rediscover that the being down deep inside is not to be feared or ugly but is glorious, beautiful, and noble. Let the Christ shine forth.

How do we do that? We must discover the Christ within. You may have heard it said, "The Christ in me greets the Christ in thee," or heard the Eastern equivalent, *namasté.* This is a beautiful concept and yet what does it mean? It is easy to throw around euphemisms, even truisms, but how do we make them real in our everyday lives? How do we take this spiritual principle from the realm of the metaphysical and bring it into the physical, bring it into our everyday lives? How do we take this somewhat global term, *the Christ,* and make it more concrete and measurable in our lives?

In Maria Nemeth's powerful book, *The Energy of Money,* she has written an exercise called "Your Standards of Integrity." In this exercise she uses an idea that has been around in New Thought circles for years. The idea is that which we see in others *with feeling* is also within ourselves. It is the concept that life is a mirror. In this exercise, Dr. Nemeth takes you through a process where you first list all the people in your life that have qualities that you admire. Now these are not talents like an artist would have like painting or playing musical instruments. These are qualities like being kind, loving, or giving. Once you have listed all of these people, then make a list of the qualities you admire in them.

Next, take the list of qualities and very deliberately and meditatively look at each quality. Which of these qualities make your heart sing? Which of these qualities warm your heart? Circle the ones that warm your heart. Next create a new list consisting of only the qualities you have circled. This is your beginning list of your standards of integrity. These standards of integrity are how you uniquely express the Christ.

What is truly in our best interest is doing the right thing—listening and following the Christ within.

This list will help you get a handle on the idea of the "Christ in you, the hope of glory" (Colossians 1:27). If you simply say, "I am the Christ," it is a beautiful idea but what does it mean in truly useful terms? With this list you now have something more concrete with which to work. You can look at your list and say, "As an expression of the Christ, I express as...." This list becomes a launching point for making this second principle more real in your life. This list will help you be the point of Power God is creating you to be. Here are some practical ways you can use it.

1. As long as we argue for our limited self we will continue manifesting and being this limited expression. So, the first way to express the Christ is to claim this truth for yourself even if this seems silly or outlandish. Here is what Charles Fillmore said about this:

> "When it dawns upon man that he has within him the primal spiritual spark of God, the living Word or Logos, and that through the Word he is

identified with the original Mind, he has the key to infinite soul unfoldment.

Even though a person does not at first have this higher revelation of his sonship and unity with creative Mind, the assumption helps him to bring it to realization." (*Jesus Christ Heals*)

"Christian metaphysicians have discovered that man can greatly accelerate the formation of the Christ Mind in himself by using affirmations that identify him with the Christ. These affirmations often are so beyond the present attainment of the novice as to seem ridiculous, but when it is understood that the statements are grouped about an ideal to be attained, they seem fair and reasonable." (*Keep a True Lent*)

Affirm what and who you really are on a regular basis. Use affirmations like these:

I am the Christ, whole, and perfect.
I am the Christ, and all is well.

If your personality or ego begins to "argue" with you, simply thank it for sharing. You could also use a denial to disempower whatever limiting thoughts you are having. Use the denial before the affirmation. A useful denial would be: *"These thoughts of limitation have no power over me."*

2. Each day, as you start your day, review your list and remind yourself how you uniquely express as the Christ. I recommend doing this as you come out of your time of meditation. Then during the day you can remind yourself periodically of these qualities, especially when you feel you are getting off track. It would be helpful to post this list where you would see it regularly like on your bathroom mirror, refrigerator, desk, and computer.

3. Setting the intention to actually practice one or more of your qualities a day is a wonderful way to bring them to the forefront. It is a way to bring your individuality to the front burner and put your personality on the back burner. You simply select one of your other qualities to focus on each day. Make it a point to express and practice that quality.

It is inevitable that someone will have a quality on their list that they do not believe is a part of them. Remember, the rule is, if you can see it in another with feeling, then it must be in you. So, for this person the seed of this quality must be present. That person only needs to exercise that quality like a body builder exercises an underdeveloped muscle.

4. You can use this list when you have a decision to make, especially a difficult one. You might think of this as your own personalized version of WWJD, "What would Jesus do?" First get still and center yourself. Then clearly state the situation in which you have to make a decision, reviewing your unique list of qualities. Next ask yourself, "What decision would a person expressing the Christ with these qualities do in this situation?" This will help you make a decision from your highest perspective ensuring the highest good for everyone.

The worksheet on the next page is to help you apply this idea:

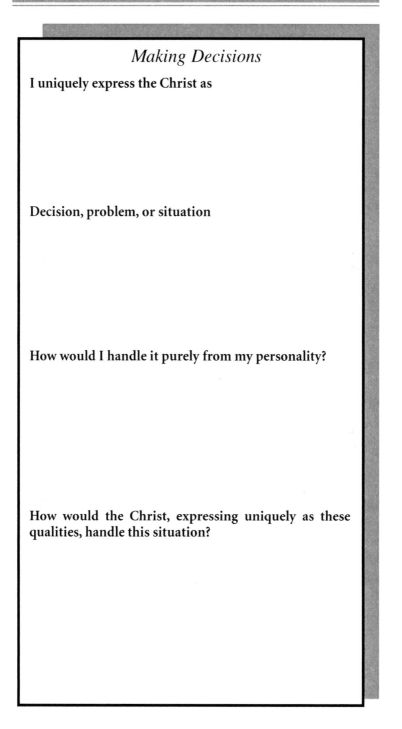

Making Decisions

I uniquely express the Christ as

Decision, problem, or situation

How would I handle it purely from my personality?

How would the Christ, expressing uniquely as these qualities, handle this situation?

5. Use this list when you have not shown up in life as well as you would have liked to; when you have acted in a way in which you feel guilty or ashamed. Center yourself and then state the situation and ask yourself, "How would a person expressing the Christ with these qualities amend, remedy, or rectify this situation?" Then listen very intently for your innate wisdom to shine forth. Now, believe me, your personality will probably not like the solution one bit. Your job is to do it anyway because you will feel great about yourself when you do.

I had a situation I created when a partner broke off a relationship. He owed me some money and was clearly not going to pay me back, even though he said he would. So, I threatened him and put him into a corner so that he would have to pay me back. I was certainly glad to get the money I was owed but not at the expense of how I felt about myself. I had stooped pretty low. In a workshop with Maria Nemeth, she helped me use the above technique to come up with a solution. Now, let's be clear, from the perspective of my personality I wanted to heap all the blame on my former partner for the way I acted. Nothing could be further from the truth, I chose to act in the way I did and it was not pretty. I asked myself, how would a person expressing the Christ with these qualities amend, remedy, or rectify this situation? The answer was clear. I needed to apologize to him. At first I wanted to say, "When you didn't pay me back and I threatened you, I want to apologize." That would have been putting the blame on him again. I came to see that I was feeling guilty for not showing up as the beautiful Christ that I am. I looked at the list of my qualities and discovered the ones where I had fallen short. Once I knew this, all I needed to say was, "When I threatened you, I was not loving, kind, or generous and I apologize for that." That's it! I simply took responsibility for my actions that were not in alignment with how I express uniquely as the Christ. When I said it, a ton of guilt lifted off my chest. And to my former partner's credit, he accepted my apology.

You see, when we are feeling guilty, ashamed, or uncomfortable inside it is not because there is a dark, ugly monster there. It is because we are not showing up in the best way that we can. We are not meeting our own standards of integrity, our own beautiful qualities of how we show up as the Christ.

Here is a worksheet to help you apply this idea:

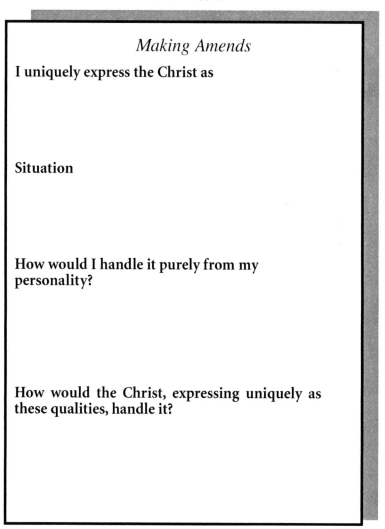

Making Amends

I uniquely express the Christ as

Situation

How would I handle it purely from my personality?

How would the Christ, expressing uniquely as these qualities, handle it?

6. The list of qualities can be used in relationships with others. If you are in a relationship, you can exchange your lists of qualities. Then, in those moments when you are having trouble seeing the Christ in your partner, you can simply pull out that list and remind yourself.

There are different ways to see the Christ in others, even if you do not have a list that they have created. You see, if each of us has the Christ within, then each of us has access to the infinite love and wisdom of the universe. Here, the principles of Attitudinal Healing come into play. When I remember that the Christ is equally within you as it is in me, I can let you find your own answers. I can choose not to see the lampshade and choose to see the lamp. I can choose to see your individuality and not your personality. I can also choose to see another as contributing to me in some way. This puts me in a generous frame of mind, receptive to the good that is present in the other.

Chapter 3

Prayer

~ Point of Power Principle ~

There have been tomes written on prayer. You can find them in any library in the country, so I will keep this short and to the point. I don't know how prayer works. I don't know why it works sometimes and why it doesn't at other times.

Dr. Larry Dossey has written several great books on prayer. He makes the point, quoting Lawrence LeShan (*From Newton to ESP*), that statistically prayers are answered in the way we want them answered about 20 percent of the time.

Now, 20 percent of the time is significant AND it is not 100 percent of the time. What is going on here? I think the point of prayer is different than what we generally think.

I liken it to an example that came to me while I was in Reno, Nevada, for the first time. I call this the parable of the slot machine. As I was checking into my hotel room in Reno, I had some extra time. I decided to play the slot machines that are everywhere present in the state. I decided I would limit my spending to $10 worth of quarters. I began to play. As I played I noticed something very interesting. I did not simply lose all my quarters one after another. No, I would lose some and win some. When I would win, the bells, whistles, and lights would go off reinforcing the fact that I had won. I would then continue feeding the slot machine until I ultimately lost all of my money. The owners of the slot machines are brilliant. They knew that I would not play if there were no chance of my winning. They wanted me to play in order to move as much of my money from my pocket to theirs. They have set up the machines so that when people play they win just enough that they keep playing and lose. It seems like you are winning or on the verge of winning until you are cleaned out. The illusion is of winning; the fact is you are going to lose as long as you keep playing.

The point of prayer is not the goodies we get but the goodness we realize we are.

You are probably asking, "What in the world does this have to do with prayer?" Like with the slot machines, the winning is answered prayer in the form that we have requested it. We don't get what we want every time because that is not the point … for God. Just like my winning was not the point for the owners of the slot machines. For God, the point is that prayer brings us into the awareness of Oneness in our creator, God. Answered prayer is the carrot that gets us to keep turning to God. Just like the winning some of the time while playing the slot machine is to get us to keep playing until we lose. However, in this case, in God's case, each time we turn to prayer we win.

In fact, we always win when we turn to prayer whether we get what we are asking for in the outer world or not. For it is in prayer that we come into conscious remembrance of our oneness with God. It is in prayer that we can step into our real power and fully realize that we are indeed created and are, in this instant, being created in the image and likeness of God.

The point of prayer is not the goodies we can get but the goodness we come to realize we are. Knowing who we are is the basis of our Power.

In the New Thought movement we pray in a very particular way. Some will say this is the only right way to pray. However, research sighted in Dr. Larry Dossey's books does not back this up. He says, "The studies I cite throughout the book not only show that prayer works, they also reveal clearly that there is more than one way to pray. A variety of methods are effective." Importantly, he goes on to say, "In the scores of scientific experiments dealing with prayer and a prayer-like state of consciousness, one of the most crucial qualities appears to be love—compassion, empathy, deep caring. Love implies letting go, venturing outside the self, breaking down the boundaries separating ourselves from others."

~ Point of Power Practice ~

The particular way we pray in New Thought is very empowering and designed to claim the truth of what we are as expressions of God. We do not pray to God, we pray from the awareness of Oneness, Godness. It is from this point of awareness we then claim our good. We claim what is already true at the level of Divine Mind, what is already true at the level of God conscious-ness. For example, if I have a health challenge, I would first center myself, becoming still and turning my attention to that place in my awareness that is peace and Oneness. This place is where all of God is becoming you and I in the most magnificent, individualized way. Eric Butterworth put it this way: "The greatest and most important discovery for any and every person is the realization that we are an 'each-ness' within the allness of God or Divine Mind...." ("You and Your Mind," in *Unity Magazine*, Nov. 1981 by Eric Butterworth)

Once I am as fully aware of this state of oneness that I can be, I then verbally claim those qualities of God that have to do with health. These would be perfect wholeness and perfect health. Then, since I am an expression of God I can know that on the level of Divine Mind I am already whole, healthy, and perfect. I then claim this wholeness to be expressing in and through every level of my being, bringing every wit of me into full alignment with the perfection that already exists. Notice that I am not hoping that it exists, I am claiming the truth of its existence right now. This entire manner of prayer is a conscious remembrance of claiming Oneness, Godness. For me, this is the point of prayer. The point of prayer is conscious remembrance, conscious awareness of Oneness, "Godness."

Here are the steps I use:

Suggested Flow of Prayer for Oneself

- **Give thanks** in advance for answered prayer.

- **Relax** and become still.

- **Center** into a greater awareness of Oneness.

- **Remember** the qualities of God that are related to the request.

- **Remember** that you have those same qualities at the level of Oneness.

- **Claim those qualities** for yourself and realize them at the core of your being. Speak words of Truth for the presenting situation.

- **Give thanks.**

- **Let go and let God**. Amen. It is done.

Suggested Flow of Prayer for Another

- **Remember** love is always enough. This helps to get my personality out of the way, which always wants to jump in and fix things.

- **Listen** to the prayer request.

- **Invite** the person into prayer.

- **Give thanks** in advance for answered prayer.

- **Relax** and become still.

- **Center** into a greater awareness of Oneness.

  Remember the qualities of God related to the prayer request.

- **Claim** those qualities for the person requesting the prayer. Realize the truth of those qualities at the core of your being.

- **Give thanks.**

- **Let go and let God**. Amen. It is done.

Here's how it might sound if I were praying out loud after having heard a request for healing:

Let us turn now to prayer, giving thanks in advance for answered prayer. We begin to become still and center into the place in our awareness where we know we are one with God. Let us rest a few moments realizing Oneness. (PAUSE.) We know God is wholeness and perfection. God is the very essence and principle of health. And, we know you and I are being created in this very instant in the very image and likeness of God. God is sourcing us now. And, so it is we know that on the level of Divine Mind you are whole and perfect. We join together claiming and knowing your wholeness and perfection, seeing radiant health as already yours. The very principle of radiant health is moving in and through every level of your being, bringing all of you into perfect alignment with the health and wholeness that already exists in the mind of God. We give thanks for these truths and that prayer is answered. We let go and let God. And so it is. Amen.

Chapter 4

Meditation

*M*uch has been written about meditation. I will briefly share what has worked for me. Often I am asked what the difference is between prayer and meditation. The stock answer is that prayer is talking to God and meditation is listening to God. For me, the lines are not always that clear. In fact, for me, meditation is not an active listening for the Presence in me to speak. Meditation is a conscious practice and technique that gets me to a point where I am dwelling in the awareness of my oneness with God. And at times I actually reach a point where I enter into what has been called the Silence, a state of stillness and peace where there are no thoughts or images. It is simply a state of being. When I pray, I usually center myself first through a short, however brief, meditation and then speak my prayer.

The technique is the container in which the possibility of going into the silence exists.

The technique I learned nearly thirty years ago was transcendental meditation. I still use it to this day. However, since that time much has been written about this technique so that one does not have to receive formal training. Dr. Herbert Benson has written two books that clearly define this technique, The Relaxation Response and Beyond the Relaxation Response. If you want a more thorough presentation on this subject I highly recommend these books. I will simply give an overview and highlights that have worked for me. This technique is sometimes called centering prayer. Calling this technique centering prayer confirms what I said previously about the blurred distinction between prayer and meditation.

This technique is not about asking for anything. It is not about actually, actively listening for anything. It is a prayer of being, a meditation of being. It is not about what we say or hear. It is about a deeper, more experiential union with God.

~ Point of Power Practice ~

*I*f you have never meditated before, I recommend starting with five minutes a day for the first week. Then increase your time by five-minute increments weekly until you reach a minimum of twenty minutes a day.

- Twenty minutes is an optimal amount of time to meditate. Once a day is good; twice a day is better.

- It is best to meditate before your day really gets rolling and sometime before you go to bed, but not so close to bedtime that you fall asleep.

Since human beings are creatures of habit, I recommend doing some things the same way every time you meditate until the practice is fully ingrained in your habit patterns. I recommend keeping as much of your environment the same as possible.

- **Choose a room** where you will not be disturbed during the meditation.

- **Set a comfortable temperature;** not so warm that you would tend to fall asleep and not so cool that you would be uncomfortable.

- **Sit in the same chair.**

- **Use soft lighting.**

- **If you like, use**
  1. Candles.
  2. Incense (of an aroma that promotes relaxation while maintaining alertness).
  3. Music (in the background and without lyrics, at a level that it does not intrude on your meditation).

- **Turn off**
    1. Your pager (unless you absolutely need to be reached).
    2. Your telephone (unless you absolutely need to be reached).

- **Ask not to be disturbed** unless there is an emergency.

What you want is to set up a situation so that when you sit down in your chair at the same time every day, everything in your environment is a cue that you are there to meditate. As the habit forms, all your sensory input will signal that you are there to meditate. This will help you slip into the meditative state faster. It is much like when doctors deal with insomniacs. They tell their patients to prepare their bedrooms in such a way as to be conducive to sleep and to only sleep in their beds. In this way, when they lie down in bed all of their sensory input is saying, "It is time for me to go to sleep."

Here are the steps:

1. Allow yourself to settle down. Do not just jump into this practice. It is best if you sit comfortably for a few minutes until you feel like you have fully arrived physically. I liken this to when a dog circles and circles and finally will lie down, adjusting itself until it is comfortable. The key here is to be comfortable and not so comfortable that you fall asleep. Use some inspirational reading as a way to settle down mentally.

   It works best to sit with your feet on the floor, hands resting on your lap, back straight in a relaxed way, and eyes gently closed. Again, the point here is to be comfortable. If, at first, you are more comfortable with your legs crossed in the manner we do in the West then please feel free to do so. I received a lot of flack about this when I first started to meditate. I was told countless times that sitting with my legs crossed blocked the energy. I finally realized that if a simple crossing of my legs blocked the energy I was seeking, then why would I want it if it were so weak? I have reached a point where I am equally comfortable with my legs crossed or uncrossed. Please feel free to adjust your posture during your meditation. Once comfortable and fully arrived where you are seated, continue.

2. Begin to turn your attention inward to that place in consciousness that is called the presence of God. The only good way to describe it is as a place of peace and calm. In a sense, at this point, you are completely letting go of any outside activities or worries and giving yourself over to the Lord God of your being...the truth of who you really are. This is a gift of your self to your Self.

3. Then begin to use a word or phrase as a tool or means to stay quietly attentive. You simply repeat the word or phrase over and over again. This can be a sacred word such as one of the names of God (Adonai, Elohim, Yahweh, El Shaddai), or other meaningful words, such as peace, love, or one. If you choose to use a phrase, keep it short, not longer than seven words. A good example would be Jesus' words, "Peace, be still."

As you use the word or phrase do not concentrate or even focus on it. That would be too harsh and counterproductive to the process. Simply use it. Allow the word or phrase to bubble up into your awareness. Simply allow the word or phrase to be there gently in your mind.

4. During the meditation you will notice, at some point, that you are no longer using your word or

phase; you will become aware that you are thinking about something else. At this point, simply
turn your attention away from what you were
thinking and allow your word or phrase to gently
bubble up again in your awareness. Return to your
word or phrase. This sequence that will occur over
and over as you meditate in this way.

I am often told when I teach this technique, "I
can't get rid of my thoughts." This is an erroneous
view of meditation. There is a generalized notion
that during meditation there should be no other
thoughts and if you do have them, you are doing
it wrong or failing in some way. What I have come
to realize is that ALL of it makes up the meditation practice. The other thoughts are part of the
meditation. They are not something to be fought
against, pushed down, or avoided in any way. That
would be counterproductive to the state of peace
you are seeking. The use of the word or phrase
and then going into other thoughts and then
returning to the word or phrase IS the technique.
It is what happens in the gap between the words
that is important. The technique is the "container"
in which the possibility of going into the Silence
exists. As one meditates, more and more, there
will tend to be fewer other thoughts and more time
dwelling in the Silence. And even this fluctuates
from time to time, even with people who have
meditated for many years.

5. When it is time to bring your meditation to a close,
   simply stop using your word or phrase. I find it
   helpful to let it go and then turn my attention to a
   scripture, prayer or other inspirational writing as
   a way to bring myself out of the meditative state.

6. Allow yourself to move around where you are seated, maybe even stretching.

7. Do not rush out of your meditation. Do not jump up right away into activity. If you do, you might find that you are grumpy or feeling off is some way. If you ever feel this way after meditating, sit back down. Begin to meditate again and come out of the meditation more slowly. This should eliminate the sense of being grumpy or feeling off in some way.

The results of meditation may be immediately felt or more likely will be felt after meditating for a period of time. I recommend using this technique for thirty days before determining whether any benefit is occurring. (See the chapter on impeccability.)

Chapter 5

Law of
Mind Action

There is the wonderful story that I wish I could give credit to from whomever I heard it. A minister is preaching about the Law of Mind Action. With great passion, he preached that the very thoughts we hold in our minds become our reality. All during the sermon the pastor could not help but notice that a teenage boy was squirming in his seat while he preached. And the more the minister preached the more upset the young man became. The minister could not wait to get the chance to talk to this young man and ask him what was up. When he did, the young, teenage boy said sheepishly, "Pastor, all I think about is girls these days. I don't want to be a girl!"

Isn't it great to know that our inner experiences of outer events don't choose us but that we choose them?

Perhaps you have heard the old cliché that whatever you *can* dream about you can become. I don't believe this either. There is a wonderful female singer at the church I attend. Now, I can dream and hold the thought with emotion that I am a beautiful, black woman singing as beautifully as this woman and it will never happen in the manifest realm. It will and does happen on the screen of my mind, but no matter how hard, how often, or how emotion filled I hold that thought, I would never be a beautiful, black, female singer.

This key idea—that human beings create their experience by the activity of their thinking—is sometimes known as the

Law of Mind Action. It is usually stated: "thoughts held in mind produce after their kind." In some metaphysical circles it is believed and taught that whatever thoughts we hold in our minds, with feeling, will eventually out-picture into the manifest realm.

Personally, I do not agree with this point of view. I know that some of the thoughts I hold with emotion do out-picture in the manifest realm. AND I am grateful that others do not!. If every thought I ever held with feeling actually manifested in this physical realm, this would be a very scary place to live!

The bottom line for us as individuals is that the law of mind action (thoughts held in mind produce after their kind) certainly operates 100 percent of the time at the level of the mind. Whatever we think about with emotion will affect our mental state.

I remember a time when I was practicing being mindful of my thoughts while I was cleaning my house in Puerto Rico. As I was walking up the stairs I caught the thought, "I'm depressed." I burst out laughing when I noticed the thought because nothing could have been further from the truth in that moment. While I don't relish cleaning the house, I was in a good mood and enjoying myself. I know if I had not caught that thought, another like it would have followed until I would have eventually been depressed.

If we think sad thoughts we experience sadness. If we think happy thoughts we experience happiness. It is as simple as that! There is now proof that our minds are hard-wired to our bodies; our thoughts produce chemicals in our body as a result of those thoughts. Positive thoughts give rise to health-supporting chemicals while negative thoughts give rise to "harmful" chemicals. Our thoughts can depress our immune system. So, it is important to watch the thoughts we hold in our minds and change them when they do not reflect what we want to experience.

I have heard some say that once one achieves or fully realizes his or her Christ consciousness then the outer events and experiences of life will all be good, that life will be easy and wonderful. This stems from the misunderstanding of the Law of Mind Action. Nothing could be further from the truth. If this were true then Jesus, as the clearest expression of the Christ, would have proven this. Since Jesus clearly demonstrated the Christ AND he had people hating him, plotting against him, and ultimately crucifying him, how then can we expect it to be any different for ourselves? We can only surmise that Jesus' experience of these events must have come from his Christ consciousness. This is certainly demonstrated from the cross when he forgives those who are crucifying him.

Sure, it can be said that Jesus was crucified because of what he held in consciousness and therefore what he taught. If Jesus did not teach his message he would have never incurred the wrath of the Sadducees and the Pharisees. However, he did not cause these events to happen to him nor did he attract them to himself. They happened because of the ideas, thoughts, and beliefs that OTHERS held in RESPONSE to him and his teachings. We, too, might expect that we might suffer the consequences of other people's ideas, thoughts, and beliefs. We sometimes reap the results or effects of other people's thoughts or ideas. They may not be necessarily ours. Scripture tells us the same thing in three different places, all quotes of Jesus:

> *"But his master replied, 'You wicked and lazy slave! You knew, did you, that I reap where I did not sow, and gather where I did not scatter.'" (Matthew 25:26).*

> *"For I was afraid of you, because you are a harsh man; you take what you did not deposit and reap what you did not sow." (Luke 19:21).*

> *"The reaper is already receiving wages and is gathering fruit for eternal life, so that sower and reaper may rejoice together. For here the saying holds true, 'One sows and another reaps.' I sent*

you to reap that for which you did not labor. Others
have labored, and you have entered into their labor"
(John 4:36-38).

Equally, it is important that we watch the words we speak for our words do have power. It is also important that we do not take this to superstitious, magical thinking extremes, laced with an unhealthy dose of fear. Many well-intentioned metaphysics students become overly fearful and vigilant about what they say. The innate Wisdom of the universe is wise enough to "get it" when we are telling a joke or being ironic.

It is important to watch the thoughts we hold in our minds and change them when they do not reflect what we want to experience.

I see this most often when students first hear about the use of the "I AM." This is a reference to when Moses said to God, "If I come to the Israelites and say to them, 'The God of your ancestors has sent me to you,' and they ask me, 'What is his name?' what shall I say to them? God said to Moses, 'I AM WHO I AM.' He said further, Thus you shall say to the Israelites, 'I AM has sent me to you'" (Exodus 3:13–14). The idea is that whatever we attach the "I AM" to we are affirming and giving power to it. If I say I am sick and tired of something then I am affirming that I AM sick and tired and then I will get sick and tired. I certainly think the native intelligence of the universe understands that to be an idiomatic phrase and it does not literally mean I am sick or tired or wanting to be sick and tired!

Truthfully, I cannot say with 100 percent certainty that we do not in some way contribute to or cause all the events that happen in our lives. What I do know is that events happen. Some of them I obviously cause; others, it appears, I had nothing to do with. I also know while I may not have control over all the events of my life, I certainly do have control over my experience of those events. My experience of an event has to do with the ideas, thoughts, beliefs, and attitudes I hold about the event rather than the event itself. Events do not directly cause my inner experience. This is really good news!

On any given day, you can hear more than one person say something like, "xyz caused me to feel abc." Nothing could be further from the truth. Events do not cause feelings. It is how we perceive, view, and think about events or comments that give rise to feelings. Think about it. If events actually caused feelings then the same event would cause the same feeling in every person that experienced the event. We know that not to be true. It is probably safe to say every person involved in an event had a distinct experience of the event depending on the thoughts, ideas, beliefs, and attitudes the person brought to the event.

Here's an example:

Let's say you enjoy going camping and your partner hates camping. If you both go on the same camping trip you will tend to have a great time while your partner will tend to have a miserable time. It is essentially the same camping trip. The event is you go on a camping trip together. Your experience and emotional reaction to the trip—enjoyment—is 180 degrees different than the experience and emotional reaction your partner is having—a miserable time.

Isn't it great to know that our inner experiences of outer events don't choose us but that we choose them? Knowing this means we can always assume the point of Power and control over our lives that we have always had: the point of Power God is creating us to be.

~ Point of Power Practice ~

What is the practical application of this principle? How can we make this principle real in the physical universe?

1. We can practice observing our thoughts. This is variously called "self-observation" or seeing your life from the vantage point of the "witness self"—that aspect of you that can observe what you are doing. It is basically true that we cannot hold more than one thought at a time. If you notice you are holding negative thoughts, actively change your thinking. Emmet Fox has written a wonderful little booklet called The Golden Key. The idea is when you notice a negative thought or that you are dwelling on something that you don't want to think about, simply turn your attention to a God thought or a God idea. An example that works for me is Jesus' words when he calmed the storm: "Peace! Be still!" (Mark 4:39). Change your thinking; change your experience.

2. There is a process that is helpful in cleaning up our thoughts. The tools are denials and affirmations. A coworker, Rev. Tom Thorpe, likes to use the word "release" in place of "denials." These are sometimes referred to as consciousness conditioners.

Denials are used to deny or release the power we have given an idea, thought, belief, or attitude. Denials are NOT used to deny an event in our lives or even a feeling we might be having. It is simply to deny that the events and feelings have any power in and of themselves over us.

An affirmation is used to state a spiritual truth about us. Affirmations are stated in the first person; they are positive statements of truth.

Affirmations are used in conjunction with denials because denials create a sort of vacuum or "space" in consciousness that needs to be filled.

Here's an example:

If you find you are having the thought like I had, "I am depressed," a denial would be, "The thought of depression has no power over me." The affirmation would be, "I am a whole and joy-filled child of God."

Chapter 6

Lessons & Misattribution

~ Point of Power Principle ~

In spiritual circles I often heard and actually agreed with the idea that life has lessons to teach me, that the universe, that God, is trying to teach me lessons. And while at first this seemed to be true, there was something about the idea that did not quite sit right with me. It didn't quite resonate with me. As I began to simply observe and watch myself, another picture, another view of lessons began to take shape; a view that was much more empowering.

As I looked back on the events in my life and the lessons I seemed to learn from them, I realized that the events themselves were not teaching me anything. They were simply events. I began to realize that I was the one choosing what lesson I would learn from any given event or situation, an important subtle shift.

In the first analysis the power is placed in the event. The event is causative. The event taught me a lesson and this lesson was determined by a power and presence outside of myself, the "Universe," God. I believe this is a misattribution of the power and the cause.

I am the point of Power; I am the one who chooses the lesson I learn.

In the second analysis, I am the point of Power, I am the one who chooses the lesson I learn. In the second analysis the event didn't do anything and there is not some external Power manipulating the universe to teach me something.

The fact is that if an event caused a particular lesson to be learned then everyone involved in that event would learn the same lesson. As I observed life I knew that wasn't true. The event might have been a catalyst but it certainly was not actively teaching any particular lesson.

Here is the example I like to use:

Let's say you love dogs and I am terrified of dogs. If you walk into a room with a dog you will want to go over and pet the dog. If I walked into the same room with the same dog I will want to run and get out of the room. It's the same dog. The dog is not causative. It is the belief you hold about dogs that causes you to go over and pet the dog. It is the belief that I hold about dogs that causes me to want to run from the room. The point of Power is not in the dog, it is in you and me.

When I was facilitating Attitudinal Healing groups for people with HIV and AIDS it was remarkable to see how people handled their circumstances. Every person in the group was in the same situation. Each of their bodies was infected with HIV. The only thing that was different was where they were in the disease process. Some of the participants handled their circumstance with an upbeat attitude. These people seemed to fare better. Others became depressed, distraught, and lost interest in living. In these people, their illness seemed to progress faster. Their circumstance was the same so the diagnosis was not causative. The diagnosis in and of itself had no power. The power was where it always was, in each individual. Each person chose his or her reaction to the diagnosis; each person chose to learn a lesson from the event or not. However, the event was not actively teaching a lesson. It was simply an event.

Similarly, but on a more positive note, we sometimes say that an AIDS diagnosis or cancer diagnosis blesses us. This, too, is a misattribution. The diagnosis/disease or event is not blessings us. As I said in Chapter One, each of us brings a blessing forth from the event. The power is in us.

~ Point of Power Practice ~

Now that we know that the lesson is not inherent in the event or that there is some external "Universe" or God trying to teach us lessons, we can be more proactive in any given situation. When an event or situation is occurring, you can simply ask yourself this question:

1. What will I choose to learn from this? or

2. What can I learn from this?

3. Also, like in Chapter One, you can ask yourself, "How can I use this for good? How can I use this to bring a blessing forth?"

4. Other questions I have used are, "How can I use this to love more? How can I use this situation to express more of God's Will which is my true Will?"

Chapter 7

Cause & Effect

~ Point of Power Principle ~

Cause and effect are never separated in the experience of life's events. Once this is realized, true change and healing can occur. Once this is realized, power is realized to be where it has always been, inside.

I am sure you have heard the phrase, "he or she pushes my buttons." Nobody pushes our buttons except ourselves. It seems when something happens, it causes a reaction within us. The ideas, thoughts, beliefs, and attitudes we hold determine our reactions and responses. When something happens, it is what we think about it (the cause) that gives rise to the reaction within us (the effect).

As long as we believe the cause is outside, we are victims of the world and we are powerless to do anything about it. In essence, no healing can occur. After all, what can we do if something happening external to us is actually causing our reaction or response? This separation of cause and effect is critical to maintaining the status quo of our personalities. This keeps us stuck in our old patterns.

As long as we believe the cause is outside, we are victims of the world.

Cause seems to be separated from the effect in two ways. Cause is separated in time or space. Cause seems to be separated in time when we attribute how we react or respond to an event from our past or future. For example, you might hear someone say, "When I was a child my mother always told me that I was bad (cause) this is why I have low self-esteem (effect)." Another way cause is separated in time is in the future. For example, you might hear someone say, "My son just got his driver's license and he might get into an accident tomorrow (cause); that is why I am worried (effect)." Cause is separated in space when an event is currently happening. For example, "What you are doing or saying to me now (cause) is making me angry (effect)." As long as cause and effect seem to be separated we are helpless to resolve the effect. We seem to be powerless because all the power is given to the outer event whether it is happening now, in the past, or in the future.

> ## As long as cause and effect seem to be separated, we are helpless to resolve the effect.

Let's look at the example where a person feels bad about herself because of how she was treated as a child. I want to be clear. *I am not saying that the events did not occur.* What I am saying is that, as a child, the girl formulated beliefs about herself. It is these beliefs in the present that cause her to decide to act in ways that reflect her low opinion of herself. The present cause is not the treatment she received in the past by her mother. Rather, the cause is a present belief about herself that is giving rise to the effect. Once it is realized that cause and effect are never separated, the point of Power is remembered to be where it has always been, inside. This is when the healing can begin. Work to heal the beliefs around low self-esteem can now begin.

In the example where the mother is worried about her son getting his driver's license, it works the same way. It is a present belief (cause) giving rise to a present effect (worry). This is not to say that concern about a child's welfare is unnatural. I am simply saying that as long as the worry seems to be caused by the possibility of her son getting into an automobile accident, cause and effect are being separated. She merely has to realize that she is the point of Power. She must realize it is her present belief that is giving rise to the present effect within her (worry). In order to heal and change her life she must realize that the cause and effect reside together.

In the example of the person feeling angry because of something somebody is doing or saying in the present moment (separation of cause and effect in space), healing can only occur when the true source of the cause is discovered to be inside, along with its effect. Here's an example. If you called me an ugly, blond woman, I would not react because I am not blond and I am not a woman. However, if I were a blond woman and believed myself to be ugly I would most likely respond or react to the comment (the effect). The only difference in the two examples is that in the first I don't believe it and in the second I do. The event, in and of itself, is not causative to my effect. It is the belief I hold about the event that causes the effect.

The key here is to remember that what is happening inside you is never an effect of an external event or situation. It is a present effect as a result of a present belief. This is why one of the twelve principles of attitudinal healing states, "We can...be peaceful inside regardless of what is happening outside." The point of Power is within where it has always been. Once this is realized, denials and affirmations can be used.

~ Point of Power Practice ~

1. Cause and Effect that seem to be separated in time

   A. Past Event

      i. Choose an event in the past about which you still have some feelings or reaction to. Journal about it.

      ii. Ask yourself, "Why do I feel this way or why am I reacting this way?" Journal your answers.

      iii. Be willing to explore the questions until you discover the inner belief that is fueling the inner effect.

      iv. If you get to a belief, ask yourself why do you believe that? Journal about that.

      v. See number 3 below.

   B. Future Events: Use the same process as above.

2. Cause and Effect separated in space.

   A. This requires being very present in the moment.

   B. Be willing to be present to the thoughts, ideas, and beliefs fueling your emotions and reactions to the present situation.

   C. Be willing to control or change those reactions until you can apply your power to the thoughts, ideas, and beliefs.

3. You can use Denials (Release) to disempower thoughts, ideas, and beliefs. Remember, when you use denials you do not deny the belief, thought, or idea. You simply state with authority that the belief, thought, or idea has no power over you. Then create

an affirmative "I statement" to create the belief you
want. For example, if you held the belief that you
are ugly, you might say this: "The belief that I am
ugly has no power over me. I am the child of God,
whole and beautiful."

Now, you will have to work with these thoughts to create a
whole new belief pattern to cancel out the old one. Also, it helps
if you act in ways to "ground" the new belief. You might go out an
buy yourself a beautiful new outfit to compliment your beauty.

Chapter 8

Clarity, Form & Intent

Y ou affirm and keep your power when you are clear
and do not confuse form with intent.

Clarity

When you are clear, you maintain your power to make
decisions that help you to be and to have what you truly
want. Clarity is important to a peaceful, centered life.
Having clarity helps in making the right decisions. When
we are clear, then whenever new information comes to us, it
comes to our clarity. This helps to further clarify our position
with regard to the new information. However, if we are not
clear, if we are confused, then new information simply adds
to the confusion.

Clarity is essential to a peaceful, centered life.

For instance, let's say you are not clear on whether you
want to have children. You meet a nice person who definitely wants children. Your lack of certainty about this will
lead to dating a person who may not be a match for you. If
you were clear that you did not want to have children, then
you would know for sure that this was not a match. If you
were clear that you wanted children, then you would know
there is a match. Since you don't know, you might date this
person for months, being not sure of what you want thus
wasting time and energy—yours and theirs.

Some people live their lives waiting for a partner or another person to tell them what they want. One always needs to be clear about what they want for themselves. Living a life while waiting for someone else to decide for you will lead to a life of stress and uncertainty. When you are clear about what you want, then you know how to consciously respond when someone else expresses what they want.

Form and Intent

During my studies of A Course in Miracles I became acquainted with the concept of the confusion between form and content. As I began teaching this concept I found that using the term "intent" for "content" made this idea more easily understood.

When you don't confuse form and intent you can be more powerful and loving to those around you. When you are clear on your intent, you use your power to decide to get what you want and need from a situation.

> Living a life while waiting for someone else to decide for you will lead to a life of stress and uncertainty.

Frequently, when we see a situation we assume the meaning or the intent behind it. This is based on our own beliefs, ideas, attitudes, and experiences. The truth is that the same form, the same action, can be motivated by very different intentions. Here's an example.

Two people can be walking down the street and pass a panhandler. One of them gives money to the panhandler out of guilt while the other gives money out of compassion. From the vantage point of a third party, the form (giving the panhandler money) is the same and yet the givers have two very distinct and different intents. This is why we must not judge by appearances. We cannot clearly discern a person's intention that motivates their actions.

When I was doing study groups in Puerto Rico, I heard a very interesting story. I wish I could credit the doctor who related this true story of an event in his life. One day, the doctor, a dermatologist, was driving through the narrow streets of Old San Juan. As he passed a corner, he saw a panhandler with a large, oozing open sore on his leg. He was begging for money.

The doctor, feeling compassion for this man's suffering, decided to help him. After much difficulty in finding a parking place, he went back to the man and handed him his business card. He told the man that he could come to his office and be treated for the sore on his leg free of charge. At this point, the panhandler became very upset and said something to the effect, "What? This is how I get what I want!" Wow, what a lesson can be learned here! Where the doctor saw suffering, the panhandler saw opportunity to get what he wanted, sympathy and money. The form was the same while the intent the doctor saw was very different from the intent of the panhandler.

We could choose to learn more from this story. I began to wonder what wounds, whether physical or psychological, I was hanging onto in order to get what I wanted. Don't we all know people who stay in situations that are not the best because of the payoff they are getting from staying in the situation? For example, a person who is co-dependent might complain about the situation yet remain because they get to stay in control.

~ Point of Power Practice ~

1. Practice, in any given situation, seeing all the different intentions that might be giving rise to that situation. Journal about it.

2. Be conscious in your own life about why you are doing anything. Have clarity about your intent. Is it life affirming? Does it support the person you want to be or know yourself to be in truth? For example,

   A. The next time you accept an invitation for a social engagement ask yourself, "Why am I doing this?"
   B. As you attend the social engagement be clear about your intention and remind yourself just before you arrive.
   C. On your way home ask yourself if your intention was fulfilled.

3. If you want a new job, be clear on what you want and how much you want to be paid in money, benefits and other options.

4. In looking for a partner for life, be clear on what you want and don't want. Then when you meet someone you can determine right away if there is any possibility of a relationship. For example, I don't tolerate cigarette smoke very well and am allergic to cats. So, I would not date someone who smokes or owns a cat. You see, I would never ask someone to give up their pet.

5. Be clear on where you want to live. For example, when we were looking for a new house in Florida we knew we needed a place that accepted two small dogs and a truck. Every time the real estate

agent suggested we "just look at" a condo that did
not allow one or both, we simply said no because
we were clear.

6. Be clear on your life vision, mission, goal, or
   purpose. With this clarified, then you can ask if
   anything you are undecided about supports it.

Chapter 9

Enthusiasm & Determination

~ Point of Power Principle ~

Knowing the difference between enthusiasm and determination will help you maintain your power so that you do not fritter away your attention and energies on projects and causes in which you have no sincere or deep interest.

Enthusiasm tends to be fleeting and passing. Frequently, projects and goals that begin in the heat of enthusiasm end up being discarded and incomplete when the enthusiasm cools down.

Determination does not give into passing whims and does not buckle under in the face of obstacles. Determination identifies the goal and doggedly moves toward it.

> Enthusiasm tends to
> be fleeting and passing.
> Determination identifies the
> goal and doggedly moves
> toward it.

I find many people have a great deal of enthusiasm and not enough determination. When a new idea or way of doing life is discovered, there is a lot excitement and enthusiasm to try it. This enthusiasm quickly wanes as time passes. If this enthusiasm is not backed up by determination then any little setback might result in letting go of the new idea or new way of living. It is easier to complete any major project if both enthusiasm and determination are present. Enthusiasm is the booster rocket that gets a new idea or way of doing life off the ground, while determination is the steady-burning rocket that provides the thrust to keep it moving.

A good example can be seen in dieting. Many people latch on to a new diet with enthusiasm. They are excited about the prospect of losing weight. However, as the day-to-day practicing of the diet wears on, enthusiasm for the new diet is lost. At this point, many give up and quit. At this point, a healthy dose of determination is important. It is the determination to stick with the diet and achieve the desired results that ensures the desired outcome.

Another example is exercise. I see it every year at my local gym. Toward the end of December the members who are there day in and day out begin dreading January as this is when all the "New Year's resolution members" start showing up. These new members show up with the best intentions and enthusiasm to begin a new life of exercise. By March most of these new members are gone. They did not have the determination to stick with the program.

Anything worth doing may get started with enthusiasm AND it is determination that sees it through to the end. The same is true on the spiritual path. A new idea, technique, or latest book may catch your attention. You begin reading the book, applying the ideas and perhaps even begin using the techniques. Then in the daily use of the ideas or techniques you grow less interested and soon stop doing it before any noticeable results are apparent or realized. I have seen this time and again with meditation. You must give meditation at least thirty days to feel and realize results. Many enthusiastically start the first week devoting their 20 minutes once or twice a day. Then life happens and reasons are found to not sit in meditation and soon they quit before they experience results. If they had backed up their enthusiasm with determination they would have achieved results that would have motivated them to continue meditating.

~ Point of Power Practice ~

1. Any time a new idea comes to mind, whether a spiritual practice, diet, exercising, or whatever, ask yourself, "Am I merely enthusiastic and caught up with the excitement of the newness of it or do I have the determination to see it through?"

2. This practice ties in very nicely with the Point of Power Principle of Clarity. You can also ask if this thing in which you are getting caught up will advance you toward your desires or goals. You can ask if it supports your vision and mission. If not, you can let it go. If the thing is tied to your mission, vision, goals, or desires, you will more likely be able to stick with it when the going gets tough.

Chapter 10

Impeccability
in your
Spiritual
Practice

~ Point of Power Principle ~

We, in a sense, misuse our power when we are not impeccable in our spiritual practice. We miss opportunities to grow and be the spiritual beings that God is creating us to be in this now moment.

I have noticed a tendency in spiritual circles to dismiss something before it is really tried. I hear things like, "It doesn't resonate with me," or "It doesn't feel right." Well, friends, the truth is, anything new just may not feel right at first. Something new may not resonate at first simply because it is new and different not because it is not for you, not because something is wrong or not right. Have you ever done the experiment where you notice for a few days how you get dressed in the morning, putting your right leg in your pants first and then the left? And then purposely, the next morning put your left leg in first and noticed how uncomfortable and weird it feels. It feels like something is wrong while in reality nothing is wrong. It is just different. The same is true with a new spiritual practice. It may feel uncomfortable, it may not resonate and it may even feel wrong at first, when in truth it is just new and different. I think we shortchange ourselves when we give up on a new spiritual practice too quickly just because it doesn't feel right.

Look at what your life is showing you.

When I was in dental school we were trained in various procedures and techniques. Frequently, these were tried-and-true techniques and usually not on the cutting edge of dental science. We would practice these procedures over and over so that when we took our board exams we would be able to do them with confidence and certainty. Also, once having learned a technique that would definitely produce a desirable outcome, we would then have that technique with which to compare any new technique. We would have a standard of comparison.

Have you ever been to someone's house for dinner and experienced a wonderful new dish, asked for the recipe, and then tried it at home? Then, while making it the first time, you decided you could improve on the recipe or change an ingredient because you did not have the one called for? What was the result? For me, the dish I made did not taste the same as the one my host provided. And then I might have said that the recipe was flawed, when in truth it was I who changed it.

Multitasking often degenerates into serial inattention.

I first heard about being impeccable with my spiritual practice in a workshop with Dr. Maria Nemeth. In our spiritual practice we frequently are not meticulous or impeccable. We frequently do with our spiritual practice what we do with new recipes. We often let our human nature get the best of us. We often cannot resist changing it to supposedly better suit us. We then wonder why we do not get the results we were expecting. Webster defines impeccable as "without defect or error; faultless; flawless."

I am inviting you to be impeccable in your spiritual practice.

~ Point of Power Practice ~

I want to invite you into another way:

A. The next time you find yourself interested in a new spiritual practice do it for at least thirty days, even if it feels wrong, uncomfortable, or not right for you.

B. Do it with impeccability. Do it exactly as you are instructed.

C. After thirty days, if it still feels wrong, uncomfortable, and not right for you or simply doesn't work, either stop it or change it. But, please, at first give it a chance.

D. Like in my dental procedures, once you know what to expect, you can then experiment with changing it and be able to compare your results.

More Power Ideas

ere are some thoughts and ideas that will help you maintain your power. These ideas have simplified my life and made my life easier.

1. Sometimes it seems that we have complex decisions to make. It is easy to get distracted by the details. The best way to cut through the complexity is to remember the simplicity of decision making. First, remember the importance of clarity and intent. Then, in the final analysis, decision making and life boil down to these two questions:

   A. Do I want this in my life? (This is where clarity and intent are important.)
   B. Who is going to get it for me?

   This may seem over simplified and I invite you to look at your life carefully. Is it not true that the first decision we have to make is whether we want something or not? Then from that decision, we simply have to determine who is going to get it for us. Often the answer is ourselves. Other times it is somebody else and sometimes it is a combination. It could even be rephrased in a less gentle way: who am I going to "manipulate" to get it for me?

   Here's an example: Recently I came home after exercising and noticed I was pretty hungry. Question: Do I want this in my life? Answer: No. What do I want? a sandwich. Now, who is going to get it for me? I could have simply made a sandwich for myself but I didn't want to make it myself. So, I asked my partner if he wanted a sandwich knowing he would "volunteer" to make it!

   If you decide you don't want something in your life I suggest you dig deeper. Usually under the "not want" is a want. The advantage of discovering "the want" is that this is something you can move toward instead of moving away from the the "not want." Certainly, going for something we want is more positive than trying to get rid of something from our life that we don't want.

For example, you could know that you don't want your current job and so want to leave it. If you leave it before you know what you want in your next job you could end up in the same situation. So, instead of first moving way from the job you don't want, you decide on the job you want and begin finding ways to get it.

Going for something we want is more positive than trying to get rid of something from our life that we don't want.

2. Another helpful hint is "to look at what your life is showing you." Now the phrasing of this implies that there is an active intelligence trying to show us something. I do not mean it like that. What I mean is that when we look at our life with an objective eye, we can more clearly see what it is we want. What we are doing in the moment must be what we really want or we would not be doing it, unless we are doing it "unconsciously" (see 4 below). This does not necessarily imply that we like what it is we are doing.

Here's an example: I had the belief that I was not into sports and was not athletic. I carried this belief from childhood when I was the last one to be chosen to play on the ball teams. I remember

I was on a date once and was asked what sports I liked. I gave my stock answer of not being a sportsman. Then I was asked what I did in my free time. I answered that I like to bike, run, do bodybuilding, canoe and others. My date began to laugh and pointed out the contradiction. As I looked at my life it was showing a sportsman and that I really was athletic! I then could drop the old belief because my life so easily contradicted what I believed.

Here's another example: I went on a trip to Palm Beach, Florida, with my friend Joyce. We met up with another friend who had moved from Puerto Rico. Like me, he was gay and along with the regular sights he was also showing us the gay bars and restaurants. At that moment I had the thought about how much I liked men. In the very next instant I heard myself ask, "Is that true?" I took that question seriously and began examining my life. I began to look at what my life could show me.

The first thing I noticed was that the only close friends I had were women. Then I noticed the only man in my life was my current partner. This did not exactly add up to loving to be with men.

I began asking myself why were there not as many men in my life as women? The answers finally came. I began to examine the early years of my life. What I discovered was that my *experience* of my father and my brothers was that they rejected me. I say "my experience" because when I look back with adult eyes I realize this was not the reality of my situation. My brothers were so many years older than I was, that "playing with me" was unrealistic. However, gym class at school reinforced my perception. I was always the last one to be selected to play on a team. Add to this the entire "women's liberation movement" where being male was sneered at or looked down on and I had quite a concoction! When I realized I was gay, this only compounded it all further.

My reaction to this, albeit subconscious, was to "pre-reject" men. Men were not in my life because of my rejection of them and NOT because of their rejection of me! I would tend to not talk with or engage the men I met at the same level I would the women I met. Even more ominous was that I think, subconsciously, I was trying to get rid of my male body when I infected myself in my dental practice.

As I realized these things, I began to work on them. I began to disempower the beliefs. When I began to do this, more men began to be part of my life and my study groups. My health also improved!

So, I used my life to point me toward beliefs of which I was not aware. This led to a life that has been more fulfilling.

3. Another behavior I see is one of indecision. Sometimes we stay in the indecision so we can have both choices. I often wondered about this, as I am usually a person who can make a decision pretty quickly.

Here's an example: One day I was really at a point where I could not choose between two good choices. The choices were: (1) going to see a long-standing friend, or (2) going for a meditation retreat. I stayed in the indecision so long that I ended up not being able to do either. As I looked at what my life was showing me, as I looked at what I did in this situation, I realized something very important. I realized that while I was in the indecision it seemed like I had both options. In reality, I had neither and ended up with neither.

4. Watch how you spend or use your resources. Maria Nemeth in her book, *The Energy of Money*, proposes that there are six forms of energy: the energy of time, the energy of money, the energy of relationship, the energy of enjoyment, the energy of physical vitality, and the energy of creativity. Often we are wasting our energy. Often we are "unconsciously" using our energy. I am inviting you to become aware in the present moment and make conscious choices about how you use your energy.

I am inviting you to become
aware in the present moment
and make conscious choices
about how you use your energy.

Here's an example: Maria uses an example of a woman who "unconsciously" spent money every day on a cappuccino to the tune of a couple of dollars a day. And yet, she did not have the money for a vacation. Two dollars a day times 352 days equals $704. That much money could get her a vacation. Knowing this, she may consciously decide to want the vacation more than the cappuccino and therefore stop buying the cappuccino "unconsciously." Each time she would want to have a cappuccino she would ask herself, "Do I really want this cappuccino or would I rather save the money for the vacation?" If the answer was that she wanted the cappuccino then she should go for it. If not, then she wouldn't buy it.

5. Another behavior I see is people feeling guilty or bad about things they hear about. This could be a famine in Africa or a war in some faraway land. I think one reason they feel that way is to *seem* like they were doing something about the problem. In reality, they were doing nothing. It would be better to remain happy and actually take some positive action to help the situation than simply feel guilty or bad about it.

6.   Lastly, multitasking is very popular these days. It is even revered as a desirable ability. Multitasking is sometimes necessary. However, what I have noticed is that multitasking often degenerates into serial inattention. This leads to mistakes and often having to re-do things.

For example, in the work place an employer will downsize to save money. This requires the remaining employees to do more in the same amount of time. Their multi-tasking increases to such a point where they do not give any one thing the attention it needs. This results in a kind of inattention resulting in mistakes, re-dos and increased costs.

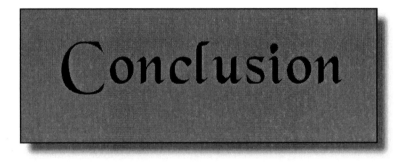

*M*y life has been quite a journey. The Point of Power Principles and their Practices have been instrumental in how I have grown spiritually. From infecting myself with HIV I have been able to create an amazing life. It is a life of giving and living more consciously. This is what these principles and their practices help us do. I trust that whatever is in your life right now, you can use these principles to create a wondrous life!

May you always remember there is only One Power and One Presence in your life, God the Good, with all your heart and all your soul and all your mind.

May you always remember God is creating you in God's image and likeness in each and every present moment.

May you always remember you are a magnificent point of Power.

May you always remember all that is God is expressing at the point of you.

May you always have the clarity, enthusiasm, and determination to demonstrate these truths everyday.

All of Divine Mind is expressing at the point of you.
—Eric Butterworth, from the cassette series
The Basic Laws of Cosmic Power

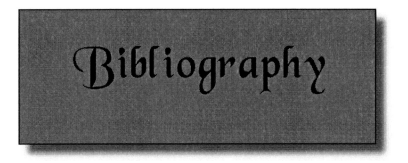

Bibliography

Benson, Herbert. *Beyond the Relaxation Response.* New York: Times Books, 1984.

Benson, Herbert. *The Relaxation Response.* New York, Morrow, 1975.

Cady, H. Emilie. *Lessons in Truth.* Kansas City: Unity School of Christianity, 1941.

Chapman, Gary. *The Five Love Languages.* Chicago: Northfield Publishers, 1995.

Dossey, Larry. *Healing Words.* New York: Harper San Francisco, 1993.

Dossey, Larry. *Prayer is Good Medicine.* New York: Harper San Francisco, 1996.

Foundation for Inner Peace. *A Course in Miracles.* New York: Foundation for Inner Peace, 1977.

Jampolsky, Gerald G. *Love is Letting Go of Fear.* Berkeley: Celestial Arts, 2000.

Kaufman, Barry Neil. *To Love is to be Happy With.* New York: Coward, McCann and Geoghegan, Inc., 1977.

Metzger, Bruse M. and Murphy, Roland E. *The New Oxford Annotated Bible.* New York: Oxford University Press, 1991.

Nemeth, Maria. *The Energy of Money.* New York: The Ballantine Publishing Group, 1999.

Trout, Susan S. *To See Differently.* Washington, D.C.: Three Roses Press, 1990.

Unity School of Christianity. *The Revealing Word.* Unity Village: Unity Books, 1997

Index